Contents

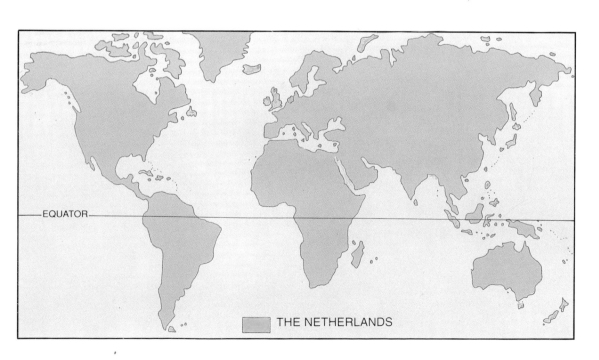

EQUATOR

THE NETHERLANDS

We live in the Netherlands

The Netherlands is on the North Sea coast of northern Europe. Many people call it Holland, but the Netherlands is the proper name. It means 'the low lands'. The Netherlands is very flat, with few hills and no mountains. Much of the land is below sea-level, so sand dunes, **dykes** and **dams** have been built to stop the water flooding it. The people who live there call themselves Netherlanders, but they are usually referred to as Dutch, which is also the name of their language.

In this book, twelve children from all over the Netherlands tell you about their lives.

Rotterdam is the largest city in the Netherlands, and the busiest port in the world.

OUR
COUNTRY

THE NETHERLANDS

Written and photographed by

David Cumming

Our Country

Australia
Canada
China
France
Greece
India
Italy
Jamaica
Japan
New Zealand
The Netherlands
Pakistan
The Soviet Union
Spain
The United Kingdom
The United States
West Germany

Cover: *Windmills are a very common sight in the Netherlands.*

Editor: Rosemary Ashley
Designer: David Armitage

First published in 1992 by
Wayland (Publishers) Limited
61 Western Road, Hove
East Sussex, BN3 1JD, England

British Library Cataloguing in Publication Data
Cumming, David
  The Netherlands. - (Our Country)
  I. Title   II. Series
  949.2073

  ISBN 0-7502-0307-2

Typeset by Dorchester Typesetting Group Ltd
Printed in Italy by Rotolito Lombarda S.p.A.
Bound in France by A.G.M.

All words printed in **bold** are explained in the glossary on page 30

ELIN
'My dad works for a diamond company'

CHANTAL
'At school I like maths lessons best'

STEPHANIE
'I spend most of my pocket money in the sweet shop'

YVONNE
'I discuss all sorts of things with my teacher'

MARTYN
'Our house is on a huge modern estate'

JUDITH
'Lots of vegetables are grown around here'

WOUTER
'It is the custom to eat a herring for good luck'

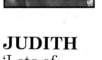

ELLEN
'The baker makes delicious pies'

SJOERD
'We burn logs in our stove to keep warm'

EDWIN
'One of our friends owns a Rhine barge'

FRANK
'Cycling is easy because there are no hills'

PATRICK
'My family is Roman Catholic'

0   50 miles
0   100 km

N

Groningen

Alkmaar

Amsterdam

THE HAGUE
Delft
Rotterdam

River Waal

Eindhoven

Roermond

The weather

The Netherlands has a **mild** climate. In most years the summers are not too hot and the winters are not too cold. There are rainy days in most months.

It is often windy in the Netherlands. Strong winds from the sea and from the north and east, blow across the flat countryside.

These modern 'windmills' use the wind to make electricity.

'We have enough logs for three cold winters.'

'My name is Sjoerd. I live in a village in the north of the country. During the cold winter months we burn logs in this stove to keep our sitting room warm. Dad chops down trees in the summer. Now we have enough logs to last us for three winters.'

'Summer weather is usually good for gliding.'

'My name is Elin. My brother Arjan is sitting in the cockpit of our dad's glider. In summer, when the skies are blue and the sun is shining, we help Dad to get the glider ready.
In winter it is too windy and cloudy, so the glider is locked up.'

Sometimes it gets very hot in summer, especially in July and August. In some years, too, the winters can be very cold; so cold, in fact, that ice forms on the **canals** and lakes and is thick enough for people to go skating.

Farming

Over half the land is used for farming. The farms are small and only a few people work on them, but they produce a lot because the soil is good and the farmers use many modern machines.

The most important farms are the ones where cows are kept for their milk, which is also used to make butter and cheese. Dutch farmers also keep pigs for bacon and grow crops like potatoes, sugar beet and wheat.

Many farmers grow flowers, which are sent all over the world.

8

Some farmers have built huge greenhouses on their land for vegetables (like tomatoes, cucumbers and lettuce). They also use their land for growing flowers, especially tulips. Many of the vegetables and plants are grown to be sold to people in other countries in Europe.

'A lot of farmers grow vegetables in greenhouses.'

'My name is Judith and I live near Delft. Lots of vegetables are grown around here in huge greenhouses. In this one, the farmer only grows peppers. When they are ripe, they are sent to the USA.'

'We keep sheep on our land.'

'I am Sjoerd. We live in the country and keep sheep on our land. Here I am feeding a lamb with bottled milk because its mother doesn't want to look after it. When the lamb is older, we will sell it at the market.'

Industry and jobs

The Dutch have always earned a lot of money from buying and selling goods to other countries. Today, Rotterdam is Europe's largest port and one of the busiest in the world.

Every day, ships unload their **cargoes** there. Some cargoes are taken on **barges** down the River Rhine to other countries in Europe. The barges return with new cargoes for the ships. Other goods are transported by road or rail. Huge **tankers** also bring oil to Rotterdam. This is **converted** into chemicals and petrol at nearby **refineries**, before being sold abroad.

Delft is famous all over the world for its pottery.

Other important industries include diamond-cutting and making all sorts of electrical machines – anything from computers to washing-machines.

'People come from all over the world to buy our diamonds.'

'I am Elin. Dad works for one of the largest diamond companies in Amsterdam. Here you can see him polishing a diamond to make it sparkle. The diamond came from southern Africa. People come from all over the world to buy our diamonds.'

'This barge goes along the canals and down the River Rhine.'

'My name is Edwin and I live in Sneek, which is pronounced "snake". One of our friends owns this barge. It is nearly 20 metres long. He uses it to carry goods along the canals of the Netherlands, as well as down the River Rhine to cities in Germany.'

Schools

All Dutch children go to school when they are six years old and stay until they are sixteen. Most go to a school run by one of the Churches. The Government gives money to these schools, and parents only pay a tiny fee.

Schools usually start at 8.30 am and finish at 2.30 pm, with a break for lunch.

At the age of twelve, children choose between going to a school which will prepare them for university or to one where they can study subjects that will help them find a job.

Children at the beginning of the school day.

'My favourite subject is maths.'

'My name is Chantal. Here I am doing sums on the blackboard. I love maths lessons, and I enjoy school. Like most schools in the Netherlands, it is run by the government, so my parents only pay a small fee for my lessons.'

'Before lessons, we discuss things with our teacher.'

'My name is Yvonne. I am sitting on the left, in the red jumper. Before we begin our lessons, we discuss all sorts of things with our teacher and everyone takes their turn at saying something. Then we all go and sit at our desks to start work.'

Most children learn two languages apart from Dutch. One is English and the other is either German or French.

Religion

Most Dutch people are **Christians**. Those living in the north are mainly **Protestant,** while those in the southern part of the country are mostly **Roman Catholic**.

There are a small number of Jews and also people from the countries once **governed** by the Netherlands, who have their own religions. They can **worship** in their special ways and **celebrate** their own religious festivals.

This church is built on high ground to protect it from floods.

14

'Most weekends we visit my brother's grave.'

'I am Sjoerd. My family are Protestant. My elder brother died a couple of years ago and he is buried here, outside the church we go to every Sunday. We visit his grave most weekends. We water the flowers and keep them tidy, to show that he is not forgotten.'

'This is the main Catholic church in our town.'

'My name is Patrick and my family are Catholic. We worship in this big church in the centre of town every Sunday in the summer. But in winter we sometimes get very cold here, so we usually go to a smaller, warmer church.'

Fewer Christians are going to church now, so some of the churches are no longer used for religious services. Instead they have been converted into exhibition and concert halls and even into homes.

Festivals

The most important festivals are connected with special events in the history of the Christian Church. Easter, for example, is celebrated with bonfires and dancing in the streets. Children hunt for painted eggs, and eat 'Easter men' made of bread.

Another happy occasion is St Nicholas's day. In the Netherlands he is called Sinterklaas (from which the English Santa Claus comes). Every 5 December he and his

The fair held in Amsterdam on the birthday of the Queen of the Netherlands.

helper, Zwarte Piet, give presents to children, and it is the custom to eat gingerbread and pastries filled with marzipan.

On 30 April the Dutch celebrate their Queen's birthday. Towns and cities are decorated with coloured balloons, lights and flags, and all schools and offices are shut.

'Here are some of the chocolate eggs I got for Easter.'

'I am Chantal. These are some of the Easter eggs I have been given. The trouble is I don't really like chocolates. But my dad and brother do, so they eat most of them!'

'I am eating a whole herring to bring good luck.'

'My name is Wouter. At the start of the herring fishing season, it is the custom to eat a whole herring to bring good luck to the fishing fleet. This is the way you should eat it!'

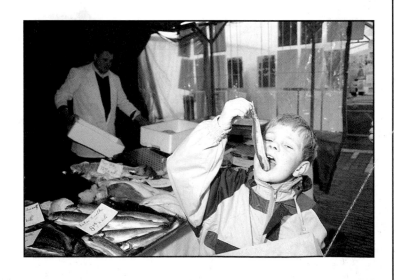

Homes

Most Dutch people live in the towns and cities, and only a small number live in the countryside. More people live in the areas around the cities of Amsterdam and Rotterdam than in any other part of the Netherlands.

In the cities you can see houses that are hundreds of years old. Some old offices, too, have been converted into smart new flats. But because the **population** has been growing, many new homes have had to be built. These are often on large **estates**

Many Dutch people live in flats. This modern block overlooks a beautiful park.

18

which have their own schools, shopping centres and parks with play areas.

The Dutch are very proud of their homes and they often leave their curtains open in the evenings so that passers-by can look into them.

'I live on a modern estate with playgrounds and parks.'

'My name is Martyn and I live near The Hague. We have a house on a huge modern estate, with playgrounds and parks. Here I am in my bedroom, catching up on some homework. The sign on my door says "Private, knock before entering".'

'My bedroom is small, so I have to keep it tidy.'

'My name is Ellen I live in a modern house in Roemond, which is in the south-east. This is my bedroom. It is very small, so I have to keep it tidy, otherwise I fall over things. I sometimes work at the desk behind me.'

Sports and pastimes

The Dutch are a sports-loving people. They are so keen, in fact, that a lot of indoor centres have been built where they can practise all year round, no matter what the weather is like outside.

In a country with so many lakes, rivers and canals, there are plenty of opportunities for water sports: fishing is the most popular, closely followed by sailing and windsurfing.

Children practising basketball at an indoor sports centre.

'I am going to save up for a horse of my own.'

'My name is Judith and I like playing the violin. Here I am practising in my bedroom. You can tell from the pictures behind me that I like horses too. Once I have learned to ride properly, I am going to save up to buy a horse of my own.'

'I once caught fourteen fish in one day.'

'I am Frank. Fishing is my favourite sport. I have just caught this fish in the canal near my home. My record is fourteen fish in one day. Most of them were too small to eat, so I threw them back into the water.'

Football is the biggest and most popular team sport, enjoyed by thousands.

Some very old sports survive in some parts of the Netherlands. In the north, for example, there are competitions to see if people can **pole-vault** over canals without falling in!

Food and drink

The Dutch like to begin their day with a good breakfast of tea (usually without milk or sugar), rolls, jam, a boiled egg and slices of cheese and cold meats.

Lunch is often a roll with meat, fish or cheese filling, accompanied by a raw herring or smoked eel from a street stall.

The evening meal may be a beef stew with vegetables or a salad, followed by a sweet pancake or yoghurt.

These porters, in their traditional clothes, are moving cheeses at the famous cheese market in Alkmaar.

'Lunch is bread with cheese, ham or jam.'

'I am Edwin. Here I am eating Sunday lunch with my parents and little sister. We eat bread and butter with cheese, ham or jam and chocolate spread. We have cold milk to drink, and mine is chocolate-flavoured. Afterwards we are going for a walk.'

'I love the special pies in our baker's shop.'

'I am Ellen. The baker in our village makes delicious pies which are special to this part of the Netherlands. They are full of different sorts of fruit. We often have a slice at mid-morning or at tea-time.'

There are many different types of restaurant to choose from for anyone who wants to go out for a meal. Indonesian ones are especially popular. Here you can order a *rijsttafel:* a selection of spicy dishes and sauces served with rice.

Shopping

The Dutch pay for goods in *guilders*. They can spend their money in modern shops or in the outdoor markets that have been held in towns and cities all over the Netherlands for hundreds of years. These markets sell all sorts of goods – from flowers and clothes to vegetables and fish.

Dutch people often buy fresh food at outdoor markets.

Parking a car can be a problem in the cities, so new shopping centres have been built outside the towns, with plenty of parking spaces. People go to them once a week, or perhaps once a month, to stock up with food and things for their homes.

'I am helping Mum to buy vegetables at the market.'

'I am Wouter. Here I am, standing behind my brother Roel. We are helping Mum to buy vegetables at the street market in the town where we live. Then we are going to visit the stall that sells sweets and nuts.'

'My favourite shop is the sweet shop.'

'I am Stephanie. Here I am visiting my favourite sweet shop. It has such a big selection of chocolates that it takes me ages to choose what I want. I spend most of my pocket money here!'

Transport

The Netherlands is very flat so it has been easy to build good roads and railways. Today the country has one of the best road and rail systems in the world. Motorways and fast trains join all the main cities, as well as linking them to countries nearby.

Many people travel by bus in the countryside and in the towns.

Because there are few hills, cycling is popular with both children and adults. There are special paths in the cities and countryside which only cyclists can use. This has made cycling very safe, so people use their bikes for many journeys – to go to school, to the shops, to visit friends and for picnics at weekends.

'Many people use the trains because car parking is difficult.'

'I am Patrick and I have just travelled home on this train after visiting some friends in town. Many people travel by train because parking is such a problem in the cities.'

'There are special paths only for cyclists.'

'My name is Frank. Lots of people have bikes in the Netherlands. Cycling is a good way to get about because there are no hills. There are paths specially for cyclists, so we don't need to go on the roads.'

Let's discuss the Netherlands

In the 1600s, Dutch sailors travelled all over the world. They traded with business people in Indonesia, South Africa, the Caribbean Islands and North and South America. Today people from these countries have come to live in the Netherlands.

Do you think this is a good thing? Does it cause any problems? Dutch traders built a town in North America and called it New Amsterdam. It is called another name now. Do you know what it is?

Facts

Population:
14,458,000
Capital:
Amsterdam
Language: Dutch
Money: Guilder
Religion: Mainly Christian

Most of the land is below sea level, so dykes are built to stop the sea from flooding the land.

There are canals even in the middle of cities.

Most Dutch children speak one, often two, other languages. How many do you speak? Do you think it is useful to know another language?

Windmills once pumped water from fields into canals.

Glossary

Barge A long boat with a flat bottom which is used on canals and rivers.

Canal A man-made waterway for ships, boats or for bringing water to crops.

Cargo Goods carried in a plane or a ship, usually to sell to another country.

Celebrate To do something to show that an event or day is special.

Christian Someone who follows the teachings of Jesus Christ.

Converted Changed or adapted.

Dam A bank or wall to hold back water.

Dyke An earth bank built to prevent water flooding the land.

Estate An area of land with lots of houses or factories.

Govern To be in charge of a country.

Mild When talking about the weather, this means that it is neither too hot nor too cold.

Pole-vault To jump over something with the help of a long pole.

Population The number of people who live in a place.

Protestant A member of one of the Christian churches other than Roman Catholic or Greek Orthodox.

Refinery A place where something is changed from one thing into another. At an oil refinery, for instance, oil is turned into petrol.

Roman Catholic A person who belongs to the Christian religion that has the Pope as its head.

Tanker A ship that carries oil or other liquids.

Worship To pray to God.

Books to read

A *Family in Holland* by Peter Jacobsen and Preben Kristensen (Wayland, 1984)

Focus on Holland by Christopher Hunt (Hamish Hamilton, 1986)

Inside the Netherlands by Ian James (Franklin Watts, 1990)

Jerry Lives in Holland by David Hampton (Young Library, 1983)

Let's Go to Holland by Chris Fairclough (Franklin Watts, 1982)

The Netherlands by Christine Osborne (Wayland, 1989)

The author would like to thank all the families who co-operated in the production of this book, especially the Hoeymakers family in Noordewolde Zuid, Friesland. Special thanks are also due to the following for their contributions: Jonathan Chambler, Hank and Hennie Kikkert, and Mariette Zoëtmulder and Anneke van Doorenmaalen of the Netherlands Board of Tourism in Leidschendam.

Index

Picture acknowledgements

Maps on contents page and page 5 are supplied by Jenny Hughes.